Seasons
of the
Narrow Gauge

A Year in the Life of the Durango & Silverton

Duane A. Smith
Elizabeth A. Green

with an epilogue by Allen C. Harper

ISBN 978-1-887805-36-0
Library of Congress Control Number: 2011934537

Duane A. Smith
Elizabeth A. Green

Photo Editor: Marc Saphir
Design and Layout: Lisa Snider Atchison
Printing: CPC Solutions

www.thedurangoheraldsmallpress.com

To the men and women of the Narrow Gauge,
past, present, and future.

Contents

Preface

Some people discover the Durango & Silverton Narrow Gauge Railroad when they're passing through Southwest Colorado. For them, it's an adventure, or an opportunity to get away from the highways and into the mountains without donning a 40-pound pack and hiking boots.

For others, it is the culmination of a lifelong dream. Perhaps they rode the train as a child, and now want to share it with children and grandchildren as they reminisce about the old days.

Still others traverse the country, riding every historic train they can reach. They know how everything works and delight in every aspect of the journey, even the rocking and swaying motion of the train.

Then there are the repeat passengers, the ones who keep coming back. They ride the train to Silverton when snow still covers the mountains, and again when golden leaves carpet the forest floor. They ride the Cascade Canyon train in the midst of a winter snowfall, and again when the snow has melted and spring is a mere breath away.

They have discovered a special magic: it is a different experience every time. Scenery changes with the seasons, but so do the sound and the feel of being on the train. From the warming rays of sun peeking through the roof of the Silver Vista in summer to the hush of a winter's day when the sound of the train whistle echoes off the mountain peaks, these repeaters want to experience it all.

They know that each ride on the Durango & Silverton is unique. There are different cars to enjoy, different locomotives pulling the train. The river changes colors. A succession of wildflowers graces the landscape. Visible wildlife changes season to season. Like a good book that can be read over and over again, the ride just keeps getting better each time.

Change is common among the people who operate the railroad as well. Brakemen become firemen and roundhouse workers. Premium car attendants work the concession car. And car barn workers help visitors in the museum. Wherever they are, whatever job they're doing, the employees have a passion for this railroad and the passengers who ride it. It shows in the square of their shoulders, the smiles on their faces as they greet each day's riders. They are proud to be a part of the D&SNGRR.

To all who work on it, ride, or simply wave as the trains go by, the Durango & Silverton is a living, breathing embodiment of history. Railroads opened the West. Durango's existence is tied to the Narrow Gauge, as much today as it was in 1881. Climbing aboard to begin the slow, steady ascent through the San Juan Mountains is like stepping back in time. The beauty of this place and the chuffing of the locomotive are all that matter.

It is an experience worth repeating – often.

Join us now to explore the seasons of the Narrow Gauge.

Acknowledgments

Many people played a role in the creation of this book. It all started with an idea of combining history with contemporary photography, to tell the story of the Durango & Silverton in a new way. John Ninnemann's photographs were combined with contributions from D&SNGRR employees and members of the Durango Photography Club. Marc Saphir ably winnowed down our choices from tens of thousands to what you see here. In the throngs of Durango & Silverton fans, none can surpass Marc for unbridled enthusiasm for this train. If we needed a photograph, he found it, or went and shot it himself. An index of photographers appears at the back of this book.

Several D&SNGRR employees added their voices to this project, both directly in the quotes you'll see and behind the scenes, by sharing their experiences, insights, and passion for what they do. Thanks to Jeff Ellingson, Charley Gremmels, Jarrette Ireland, Robert Manore, J. Leigh Mestas, Mike Nichols, and Greg Simpson for sharing their observations on working for the railroad. And special thanks to Yvonne Lashmett, who not only shared her experiences with the railroad, but also searched until she found what we were looking for time and again, always with patience and grace.

It takes a skilled, creative designer to wrestle so many elements into a cohesive, beautiful whole, and no one does that better than Lisa Atchison. Her award-winning, artistic eye was crucial in the selection of photos, and even more so in putting it all together.

And special thanks to Al and Carol Harper, who wrote about their vision for the future of the Durango & Silverton, and placed their full confidence in Durango Herald Small Press to produce a book to complement that vision.

– **Duane A. Smith**
Elizabeth A. Green
Durango, Colorado
Summer 2011

Prologue

The Key to the Promised Land

"The town without a railroad is no town at all" could summarize the role and significance of the railroad in the second half of the nineteenth century. Railroads presented communities with a promising future. They could just as easily kill that future if they bypassed a village, a fact that caused some settlements to pack up and move to a new site nestled by the tracks. Some railroads even built communities, particularly in Colorado, where the Denver & Rio Grande Railroad held sway.

Living in the West, where distances were measured in time rather than miles, it was essential for the farmer, rancher, miner, merchant, and all their contemporaries to connect, in some form, to a railroad. The railroad provided the fastest, easiest, most comfortable, year-round, and probably cheapest way to get hither and yon.

The railroad, more than anything else, opened the West and made it accessible to settlers, tourists, and all others who came out to "see the elephant," as folks loved to say.

Nearly free land awaited the hard-working, ambitious farm family, under the federal government's generous Homestead Act. For the aspiring merchants, brand new towns along the railroad tracks offered opportunities unknown in the more settled region of the country. Railroads moved ore from mines to smelter/mill and goods from eastern warehouses to western merchants' shelves.

Indeed, the railroad fathered the tourism industry. Now it took only days, instead of weeks or months, to go from the Midwest and East to reach this promised land of beauty, wonders, and scenery unimagined. The West offered it all, and the railroads bought into the concept and became the tourist agents of that generation.

The wonders did not stop there. Colorado particularly beckoned as a health seekers' mecca. At a day and time when consumption was deadly, fevers and ague bedeviled young and old alike, and aches and pains made life miserable as one grew older, the miracle answer to them all could be found in hot springs. Colorado offered them in spades, and they promised to cure almost any ail-

Bob Trennert

Daily Silverton train departs Durango June 13, 1963.

ment known to mankind. They promised also, sadly, to offer relief for ailments to which there was no known cure. For the desperate health seeker, however, they might offer a last hope.

Not only that, Colorado's pure, ozone-filled, non-humid, mile-high air promised relief for one and all. One's health and general outlook would improve almost instantly upon arrival in this mecca.

How did one reach this land of wonders and new life? The easy answer was the railroads, which made it possible, in fact had to make it possible, so they could earn profits. That was why time, planning, energy, and money had been spent to survey, build, and develop the network of railroads that moved from east to west. In the case of the first transcontinental railroad, it was built from both directions, east and west, toward the middle. When all was said and done, a network of iron rails crisscrossed the West by the 1890s.

America led the world, during these amazing decades of railroading, in cheering on the iron horse and all the benefits it promised to bring. Its development of new cars, more powerful train engines, track-laying methods, and a host of other ideas and improvements amazed the world. Certainly, the industry was helped by having huge amounts of unsettled land available, which meant not having to cross a national boundary with all its concurrent problems. The federal government definitely assisted by generously giving away land beyond the Missouri River and paying bonuses to encourage railroads to build into the unsettled West.

Potential settlers found the railroads to be a bonanza of pamphlets, materials, and promises about what awaited them in the "promised land." They also found encouragingly cheap rates to get there. Their benefactors even hinted that rain followed the plow, the iron rail, and the telegraph line. Somehow, these would tickle (electric currents!) the clouds and bring rain to the normally semi-arid Great Plains region.

Railroads pushed and boomed urbanization. Everyone benefited, and coincidently the railroads made money much to the joy of stockholders. Maps of railroad lines show how the towns were separated by five or ten miles, which allowed farmers not to have to travel too far to reach shipping facilities.

It all benefited America and in those years between 1865 and 1900, the West was opened, settled, and developed. By the century's end, nine new states had joined the union and two territories awaited admittance. Without the railroad, much of this advancement would have been delayed. A host of natural resources would not have been developed, a western epic would have been short-circuited, and the United States would not have become one of the world's powerful nations.

Americans loved their railroads. They wrote, sang songs, described trips, took photographs, and painted pictures of and about them. Yet there was a dark side in all this. Unregulated in this era of big business dominance, railroads did what they felt like doing to make profits, sometimes excessive. They ran their trains at their convenience. They demanded concessions from towns and counties, and threatened to go elsewhere without them.

They fought with each other and often gave no quarter. Then they became monopolistic. Sometimes they had a "public-be-damned attitude." Trains might be the best and fastest way to go from here to there, but they could be unsafe. They might offer low prices and easy terms to transport homesteaders to the West, but once there, they were under the railroads' thumb, from freight rates to storage facilities.

All this led to unhappiness among westerners. By the 1880s, they had had enough. Various groups protested, organized, and made railroads one of the chief villains in their political uprising, the populist movement. As one speaker shouted, they should "raise less corn and more hell" – and they did. Western newspapers, politicians, speakers and agitators blamed the railroads for a host of problems, some of them justifiably so. The benefactor had become the villain.

This, then, was the railroading world of the last generation of the nineteenth century – a world of hope and despair, of good feelings and bad, of profits and failure, and of promises made and expectations not met. With great expectations and anticipation, William Jackson Palmer brought his Denver & Rio Grande Railroad into this world.

Colorado's baby railroad would play a role in expanding the state, just as Palmer ardently believed it would, and would particularly play a major role in opening and developing the state's southwestern section.

"I love the railroad because it is a piece of history we can still see, touch and experience. It takes you back to the glory days of railroading and keeps a part of that alive and available to us."

– Charley Gremmels
Employee since 1987
accounting department

Chapter 1

A Dream Becomes Reality 1870s-1960

The story of the Denver & Rio Grande Railroad is the story of one man's dreams and their realization – William Jackson Palmer. A Civil War veteran, Palmer had been born in Leipsic, Kent County, Delaware, on September 17, 1836.

Following the war, Palmer, who had risen to the rank of brigadier general of volunteers, looked for opportunities in the expanding post-war boom. Already an experienced railroad man, he seized the opportunity to join the Kansas Pacific to scout the route west, which brought him to Colorado Territory. He became fascinated by the possibilities that southern Colorado offered and in 1869 went east and on to England, searching for financial support for his own railroad. British investors, who had smaller gauge railroads than their American cousins, liked the three-foot narrow gauge idea.

He found the finances and the Denver & Rio Grande was born. His plan was novel. Rather than ask for large government land grants, Palmer sought just the right-of-way so that he could develop communities along the way. Part builder, part utopian dreamer, he fell in love with a site at the foot of Pike's Peak. There, he would organize and promote Colorado Springs.

Construction on the railroad began in July 1870 and by mid-October the line had reached his new town. Instead of saloons, Colorado Springs would have "genteel refinements," and be "the one spot in the West where nice people could gather together and live out their days in gentility and peace."

The 1873 crash and subsequent depression slowed Palmer's plans and then the Leadville silver boom pushed him into the mountains at the perfect time. Silver discoveries were being made everywhere in the new state.

One of Palmer's most amazing projects in the years that followed was building a line into the heart of the silver-ribbed San Juan Mountains at Silverton. To the astonishment of many, Palmer decided to swing south along a 245-mile route over some of the most rugged terrain yet challenged by an American railroad. It would dip into New Mexico numerous times, climb over Cumbres Pass (10,015 feet), and then finally reach the Animas Valley, still fifty miles short of

Duane Smith collection

Durango, late 1880s

its destination.

Here, the railroad built Durango, after older Animas City failed to agree to terms that the railroad demanded to make it the railroad hub. The older community never recovered and sixty years later joined its upstart and now much larger neighbor.

Durango, the "new wonder of the southwest" became the railroad and coal mining center for the neighboring silvery San Juans. Meanwhile, the railroad pushed on, reaching Silverton in July 1882. It proved a major construction project.

The major problem loomed on the cliff a few hundred feet north of Rockwood, the end of the line in 1881. From there, cliffs dropped off "more or less"

"civilization and progress in the remote fastnesses of the mountains"

Newspaper publisher Caroline Romney wrote in colorful detail about her visit to the workers' camp and construction of the narrow gauge railroad from Durango to Silverton along the Animas River.

The location is charming, and so sheltered that although the altitude is about seventy-two hundred feet, the men have not suffered from cold during the winter and have worked regularly every day. The sun beats down into this little woodland retreat with a spring like intensity, which is increased by reflection from the rocky heights around and everything is so cheerful and pleasant as to rob "roughing it" of all its terrors and the bountiful table, set by the little cook, makes one sigh, to live always in this wilderness.

Over the brink of it,
Picture it!
Think of it!

The seething waters and rugged rocks below, the broken and mangled limbs, and yet these railroad laborers, unsung heroes, work here day after day, taking their lives in their hands on the icy crags above this abyss, where death yawns for them if they make but one false step. Thus do they make civilization and progress possible in the remote fastnesses of the mountains, and unlock the hidden treasure-houses of Nature to the commerce of the world.

The *canon* extends in box form for a distance of about three miles, beginning about a half mile above the camp.

For a distance of fifteen hundred feet, they have to cut the side of the *canon*, down so as to form a road-bed, sixty-five feet below the top, and for two thousand feet, they have to make cuts to the same depth through the sides of the cliffs, in order to get out of the *canon*.

The cliffs also have to be cut down for a mile and a half above this section, although not to so great a depth, and above the rock work continues all the way to Silverton, a distance of twenty–four miles. . . . all told [a distance] of thirty-three miles of continuous rock work in a line less than fifty miles long."

[The canyon and the river] do not follow a straight course by any means, but wind in and out among the mountains in the most tortuous fashion, affording constant and bewildering changes and the most unique and surprising outlines entitling this region to the appellation *par excellence* of The Switzerland of America.

. . . nature seems to have had an eye to the future when she opened up 'This Great Chasm' through the mountains and to have known that the railroad builders of the nineteenth century, with all their cunning and enterprise, would need her assistance. They could not afford to do what she, in her slow processes, had been a million years in doing, but they can supplement her work with the assistance of giant powder and electric batteries, and knock down the sides of the mountains still more, until they can gain a foot-hold in their sides.

In the earlier work on the canon, the men had to be let down from the top by ropes to drill the holes for powder, but now they have made their pathway along the face of the cliffs and can proceed with their labors, in a less hair-raising fashion, although when a hundred kegs of powder were touched off the entire mountain [shook] for a moment.

The constant cononading [sic] of the blasts among the rock, now near, then farther off, was something grand and far more satisfactory than listening to the din of a battle afar off, for its victories are not only bloodless but certain, each report being a signal announcing another great advance in a work, which is one of the triumphs of peace.

The debris from the work, chokes the river in places to such an extent as to have raised its bed several feet, damning it up and rendering it still more furious in its foaming rage. No wonder it is angry at thus having the work of centuries imposed on it over again.

The work done by the company along this *canon* is probably the most wonderful of any on its wonderful line. Mr. [Thomas] Wigglesworth who located the line and has superintended its construction up to the present time, has reason to be proud of this triumph of his skill, and deserves unlimited credit for the masterly manner in which he has executed the trust confided to him. Probably no where in the world is there so long a reach of such difficult work. When completed this road will afford a panorama of beauties.

Denver & Rio Grande train on Highline near Rockwood, circa 1890.

La Plata County Historical Society

Durango & Silverton Narrow Gauge Railroad

Snowslide near Silverton, circa 1930.

about 400 feet from the top directly into the Animas River. This would become the famous Highline. Blasted out of a sheer rock wall, it was an engineering and construction wonder. Miners dangling over the cliff blasted out the right-of-way and from there the route to Silverton became easier.

Caroline Romney, editor of the *Durango Record* provided the best firsthand account of building the railroad. On a visit to the construction camp in February 1881, she encountered "railroad contractors…who are doing the heaviest work on the line, having a contract for grading one mile for the sum of $70,000." When she reached the main camp, she saw "one side opening out to the brink of the canon." She described five subsidiary camps that supplied 300 men, "quite a little

village" of log buildings. It was, she wrote, a "pleasantly comfortable" railroad camp.

Costly, time-consuming, and dangerous, the Highline reportedly cost Palmer $1,000 a foot. By the end of the year after finally overcoming this major obstacle, the D&RG moved ahead with powder men, graders, and tie cutters feverishly working while Silvertonians continued fussing. Their work included a 150-foot bridge across the Animas River that further slowed advancing toward Silverton, until it was finished early in 1882. Taking this construction all together, it was considered one of the engineering marvels of the day, one that brought engineers to study it.

Durango & Silverton Narrow Gauge Railroad

With the completion of the road, Silverton celebrated, Durango celebrated, and mining prospered. In the years that followed, the Denver & Rio Grande persevered through the "best of times, the worst of times." Winter weather posed problems, then the collapse of silver mining in the 1890s ended one financial pillar, just as tourism started to forge another.

As the twentieth century dawned, the D&RG and railroading in general witnessed their last hurrahs. A gradual decline set in as the old-fashioned steam lines faced competition from the Model T and lighter-than-air craft. But the line from Durango to Silverton chugged on. Mining reached it peak by 1908, and agriculture limped along. The times they were a-changing.

World War I came, along with government control of the railroad, and then the country entered the "roaring twenties." Meanwhile, the railroad started to enthusiastically push tourism. But alas, the San Juans did not receive their just due. The 1922 Denver & Rio Grande Western (as it was now named) published a guidebook in 1922 about the wonders of touring along its line. Durango and Silverton, not being on the main line, received only one mention between them. Nor did the "roaring twenties" roar in southwestern Colorado.

With the stock market crash of October 1929 the country slipped into the century's worse depression. The railroad moved to suspend operations on the revenue-losing Silverton line, an action that quickly prompted locals in both communities to jump to the barricades in protest. Joined by Durango merchants and others, they succeeded in preventing the closure of the route. Yet the threat hung over the line.

World War II came and went. After the war railroad lines were abandoned right and left in Colorado and elsewhere as passenger and freight traffic steadily dropped. Still, the Durango to Silverton continued to operate, though somewhat as a forgotten segment of the railroad. But its days seemed numbered. "You can't run a railroad on sentiment," observed a D&RGW official. Trains to Silverton now generally included only one passenger car, a freight car or two, and a caboose.

The line did gain a moment of fame in the 1950s and early sixties, thanks to Hollywood. However, more than the narrow gauge train attracted Hollywood moviemakers. The appeal of the spectacular scenery that lured them into the area must also be added to the attraction. All told, everything proved perfect for those popular western movies. Among others, *Ticket to Tomahawk, Denver Rio Grande, Around the World in Eighty Days, How the West Was Won,* and *Butch Cassidy and the Sundance Kid* were shot in part featuring the rail-

Durango & Silverton Narrow Gauge Railroad

Silverton, looking west along Greene Street, with Town Hall on left. Date unknown.

Facing page: Arriving at Silverton, six cars, 20 mph, June 4, 1940.

road and the scenery.

The Hollywood era ended for several reasons. The railroad repeatedly commented that "it was not in the entertainment business" and, eventually, seemed to grow tired of all the hassle and commotion. Nor did a large number of film plots exist that could utilize trains, mountain scenery, and two western communities, without repeating of plots, themes, characters, and locations.

As the 1960s opened, the Durango-to-Silverton segment of the railroad had escaped abandonment, as had its Alamosa connection to the rest of Colorado. That perhaps represented the best that could be said. Pleas from the Durango Chamber of Commerce, Silverton, La Plata and San Juan county commissioners, and "influential citizens," including both Colorado senators, helped save the line.

As the 1960s opened, its future still remained in doubt. Loyal people supported the little train, but times had shifted against railroading. What the future might hold, no one could really tell.

Chapter 2

Steaming into the Tourist Era 1960s-2010

As the post-war years dawned, southwestern Colorado and the whole state entered a new era. The economic base of earlier decades – mining, railroading, agriculture – was either nearly gone, less important, or severely declining. The new Colorado base would be tourism, higher education, high-tech industries, federal, state, and local government, and a continuation of the concentration of wealth and economic opportunity along the Front Range, from Fort Collins to Pueblo.

This left the hinterland with few opportunities. Fortunately, southwestern Colorado offered tourism and soon, a four-year college. At least, Durango did. Silverton sat on the outside looking in as the new era dawned. Mining continued to support the town's economy, with a revival sparked, in the 1960s and 1970s, by the Standard Metals operation. It lasted into the 1990s, but looked nothing like the old days. The miners generally lived and shopped in Durango, Montrose, and Ouray and commuted to work. Silverton's population fluctuated on a downward curve and its business district grew smaller and smaller. Sadly, the railroad participated little in this last mining hurrah. The hauling of freight was much more feasible, timely, and economical, in and out of Silverton and Durango.

Both communities had something that offered great tourism potential – a narrow gauge railroad that ran through some of the most spectacular mountain scenery in all of Colorado. Enthusiasts claimed that it was one of the "best" trips in the whole world. It might be only a mixed train, of passenger and box cars and a caboose; nevertheless, it continued running in what were otherwise "down" times for railroading. Fewer passengers and less freight, however, raised questions about the line's long-range future.

One small segment of those passengers, though, hinted at change. They rode the train because they were railroad buffs who enjoyed steam railroading and appreciated the train's historic significance. Others rode because of the spectacular scenery along the way. For them all, the Durango to Silverton train represented something special to be savored, so if at all possible, it must continue to operate.

The Denver & Rio Grande Western Railroad owned a potential tourist bonanza, but failed, at the moment, to appreciate it. From The Denver & Rio Grande Western's perspective, the Silverton line lingered on as an unprofitable relic from a bygone era. It produced little, if any, profit, and offered no realistic monetary incentive for converting to standard gauge.

The company persisted in saying that it was not in the entertainment business. Railroad officials appeared to believe that if the narrow gauge line ignored passenger traffic, supporters would become discouraged and disappear. Abandonment, then, would be the logical move, and, from the railroad's point of view, the "convenient end result." For decades, the D&RGW had been abandoning one unprofitable narrow-gauge segment after another. Until now, the Silverton line represented nearly all that remained of the once extensive, legendary system into the mountain mining districts.

Furthermore, its connection segment, the Alamosa-to-Durango line, with its Farmington branch, presented few future profitable opportunities. Trucks had carried the day. The D&RGW in southwestern Colorado and northern New Mexico appeared a prime prospect for abandonment by the late 1950s.

What kept it active for another decade, though, was the oil and natural gas boom in the Farmington area in the 1950s and early 1960s. The railroad already operated into that area and could carry heavy equipment and supplies more easily than trucks. Lumbering helped keep the line going as well, but the trucking business cut in everywhere else.

The handwriting seemed to be on the wall when the D&RGW had suspended passenger service between Alamosa and Durango in 1951. It did so over the objections of southwestern Coloradans, some of whom attended abandonment hearings in Alamosa. They testified how much the railroad meant to the region, but lost their case completely when they admitted that they had driven their cars to the meeting instead of taking the train on its slower, round-about, route.

In the following years, despite local hopes, freight business failed to provide enough profit. So abandonment occurred all around Durango in the decade of

Bob Trennert

A train filled with happy tourists passes the Hermosa water tower ahead of an approaching storm, August 1965.

the sixties. The Durango-to-Farmington and Alamosa routes were abandoned, over the strong protests of local residents and officials.

The Interstate Commerce Commission authorized the abandonment of freight service in July 1969. There was, the commission said, "no substantial demand, for the freight services, and shippers presently using the line" that could not be "adequately met through available trucking service." Among factors the ICC cited were the "continued money losses largely attributed to weather conditions" that hampered winter operations.

The *Herald,* in its Colorado Day editorial (August 1, 1969), expressed some of the local concerns: "The greatest fear concerning the abandonment has been that Southwest Colorado would be subject to the much higher trucking rates. Rio Grande officials [have] said repeatedly that the railroad could make no agreement on freight rates." The editorial continued:

> The D&RGW's narrow gauge to Silverton is Durango's outstanding tourist attraction. The publicity it receives across the country brings many people here, even some who do not ride the train.
>
> It's proper that residents should be concerned about any plan which might have an adverse effect on The Silverton. It's proper too that others in the Four Corners area take no action which damages one of the towns in the area. The Silverton is a big help in keeping Durango and surrounding towns on their economic feet.
>
> There's nothing in the ICC order to prevent another attempt to abandon The Silverton. However the profits are a barrier . . . The train does represent a sensitive spot. Durangoans have good and valid reasons for caring greatly about the welfare of the operation.

Finally, after decades of worry, an epochal link to Durango's past had been broken. Only the Silverton segment continued running. For that, Durangoans could thank some of their neighbors who had taken up the cause, as well as Silvertonians and their own efforts.

The D&RGW did win one round of the ongoing saga. It achieved a ruling from the Interstate Commerce Commission that it need not operate from October until the start of the next tourist season. Nor did it any longer have to carry freight. Each step seemed to inch the line nearer to abandonment.

The railroad's management might have been considering surrendering to the changing times and bowing out completely. But some passionate employees on the Durango-to-Silverton run had thought otherwise for years. The station agents, conductors, brakemen, engineers, and firemen worked endlessly to entice passengers on their own and spread the word about the trip's scenic and historic attributes.

They had started promoting the concept in the forties and, gradually, it had worked. In 1947, for instance, nearly 3,500 people rode the train, a figure that by 1953 had jumped to over 12,000. They were gaining supporters as well as riders. Durango and Silverton businessmen and women also began to see the trip's value, adding another local attraction and thereby potentially increasing the numbers of tourists coming into the region.

Looking back over those years, station agent Amos Cordova laughed about the times the Rio Grande officials wondered how 400 people were riding a train that supposedly held only 300. He always told them he did not know, but "we had our ways of putting people on there."

Interest actually revived at just the right time. Across the country, people were becoming aware that a railroad heritage, the steam locomotive and its lonesome whistle, were disappearing, along with an era in American history. In its place came the diesel engine, efficient definitely, cheaper to operate certainly. But romantic, with a railroad heritage? Never.

Conductor Alva Lyons deserved a great deal of the credit for being a staunch advocate and arousing public interest in saving the Durango-to-Silverton train. Remembering those days, he told how he carried excited travelers in the caboose, or in a freight car that had a baggage compartment, when the regular train had no passenger cars. It was, he recalled, a homey situation, but passengers enjoyed the experience of steam engine railroading as well as the scenery.

"We always served coffee to any passengers in the caboose; that was the start of it, and I didn't actually start serving coffee in the big coffee pots until I was conductor on the passenger train," recalled Lyons.

Amos Cordova remembered 1950, when he began working for the D&RGW. "Some of the rail fans discovered that this little train was still running, so I started working through them, through word of mouth." With diesels in the present and future, "steam was beginning to be taken off a lot of major railroads," and time was running short for the "past."

In one tradition that endured, all new station agents and other officials had to purchase a Hamilton pocket watch. The railroad sent down a "clock official" on a regular basis to check the watches to be sure that all were running correctly. When Cordova retired after forty-eight years, his prized watch continued to keep good time.

As the fifties slipped away, the idea of a railroad trip was catching on. *Durango Herald* publisher Arthur Ballantine noted in a July 3, 1957, editorial about Independence Day, that in addition to participating in the patriotic celebration, "hundreds" would be riding the narrow gauge. The railroad joined with Mesa Verde, picnicking, fishing, and playing softball as one more way Durangoans would make the holiday a "festive day."

Supporters continued to keep up their determination to save the scenic route and its nostalgic journey. Slowly but surely, they were joined by others – but not the railroad. The D&RGW continued to insist that it was not in the tourist business, nor was it intended to be. As short-sighted as that might sound today, it did make sense in the late 1950s and early 1960s.

In the meantime, Colorado banker William White, who had recently purchased Durango's First National Bank, tried to buy the line in the early 1960s, after the announcement that the railroad planned to abandon the line. It was "badly handled," recalled bank official Robert Sawyer, and the plan went downhill after a luncheon meeting.

Bill announced the D&RGW was going to abandon the railroad and to keep that from happening he had started a foundation, the White foundation, to perpetuate the railroad, as a non-profit foundation.

There were people from Silverton and Durango there and there wasn't too much said at the luncheon, [that were] objections. At that time the mining company, Standard Metals, was the second largest taxpayer in the county and sure as heck didn't want to be the largest. So they got the word out that if the railroad were out of D&RGW hands, there would be no way to ship the ore out. Well, the ore was going by Ouray to Montrose by road to be loaded on trains anyway.

The reaction proved swift. "[The First National in] one week lost well over $1 million in deposits from San Juan County. It was really unfortunate. It was out of consideration and concern for Durango and Silverton that he wanted to buy the railroad." The line's "perils of Pauline" continued.

A group of Durango businessmen then moved to buy the line. Their effort came to naught as well. So the D&RGW continued to operate "the journey into yesteryear" as an unwilling "parent."

One can understand why President Gale "Gus" Aydelott wished to sell. Railroad business continued to decline. The entire Durango-to-Silverton line stood alone as narrow gauge, and it was costly to run tourist trains with an unknown potential, possibly at a loss for the hard-pressed D&RGW. No uniform agreement existed, however, among the railroad's management. Some executives wanted to keep the line; they "loved it." For example, they sent some of their high-priced clientele to Durango to ride the Nomad so they would know "what the narrow gauge" was all about and enjoy the trip's scenery.

With Aydelott stood those who feared rising costs, replacement of aging rolling stock, rock slides, and weather-related problems, as well as roadbed and track maintenance. The railroad's present and future prospects did not appear to warrant such an economic gamble. To them, the "klickety klack," as they called it, needed to be abandoned.

Against them though stood another group, those people who thought the line held great tourist potential. Railroad employees were counted among that number. In 1961, for example, they sold railroad spikes for $1 each to raise money to fund an attorney to fight abandonment.

Also, merchants in both communities did not want to lose what potentially could be a tourist bonanza. Railroad buffs and others who did not want to see this piece of Americana disappear joined them in the attempt to preserve the Silverton line. The two sides sparred and watched each other with jaundiced eyes throughout the sixties and into the seventies.

Ballantine, owner and editor of the *Durango Herald*, recalled those days in a 1974 interview:

> The narrow gauge train was just beginning to be discovered in the 1950s and the railroad was resisting it. They wanted to take it out of circulation. We did a great many things [to save the railroad]. The editorials really weren't so important as the politics – getting our senators and representatives [involved].

Ballantine continued on the subject, adding a bit more information on White's attempt to buy the line.

> [He] endeavored to set up the Helen Thatcher White Foundation to buy the railroad. Then the Silverton people threw this out because they simply wanted the D&RGW to continue as a train. The whole thing may not have been handled in the best possible way, but anyway, at the abandonment hearing, because the train was making a profit on the books – which we all knew – abandonment wasn't granted D&RGW.

Ballantine went on to explain why, in his mind, they wanted to abandon, or sell, their little line – "because they are freight minded."

President Gale Aydelott reinforced that view, pointing out, "You are less than one percent of our revenues." It was then suggested that the National Park Service run the line. Ballantine had his doubts.

It's been suggested, but not seriously enough for us really to think about it. I'm not certain how well the National Park Service runs things of this order. It's got to be run well and maintenance is a problem on a train. You've got to have somebody with capital. You're going to have floods in that Animas Canyon – and we've had them – so you can't get some fly-by-night [operator].

Despite the corporate desire to abandon the line, the D&RGW had planned and carried out an "urban renewal" project for the area in and around the depot, at the end of Main Avenue. It all started when Alexis McKinney arrived in Durango in 1963 to manage the Silverton branch. Among the problems he faced was the depot area. Over the years, it had become a rather depressed neighborhood, featuring a good many bars. That did not provide the best introduction to the "ride into yesterday" for families, or anyone else.

McKinney had a keenly tuned appreciation for history and preservation, and an abiding determination that steam would be king of the Durango-Silverton route, as it always had been. Even though the D&RGW didn't share his view of the railroad's potential as a tourist attraction, he had enough latitude in his job to pursue his vision.

He set about to create something special for tourists and the railroad. At the same time, though, he did not want to push the concept too far. A proverb on his office wall said it all: "Beware, lest love of the antique lead to lamentation over progress."

While in charge for not quite three years, McKinney demonstrated that the railroad business and tourism need not be irreconcilable. The concept of "Rio Grande Land" included a cleanup of the area and having the district around the depot focused more on tourists and families. The depot itself changed drastically. Gone were the telegraph office, the baggage room, and the offices. The ticket office expanded and the depot's north end became a waiting room and gift shop. The restrooms were moved from the outside to inside the building, and the offices were now located upstairs, out of the tourists' way.

Buildings in the neighborhood were renovated or torn down, to be replaced by Victorian-style structures. Businesses opened, aimed at garnering the tourist dollar. The center of focus, though, remained the 1882 depot and the train that provided the "door into the past."

As early as 1963, the "just started" Rio Grande Land was being touted as one of Durango's best tourist attractions. The *Herald*, in its special "Southwest

Tourists wait to board the Durango & Silverton at the Durango depot, summer 1977.

In his 16 years as owner (1981-97), Charles Bradshaw transformed the Narrow Gauge into a linchpin of Durango tourism.

Colorado" edition (April 1963), introduced the concept to its readers.

The nostalgic tourist trip on a steam train through beautiful mountain scenery and a stunning canyon was catching on with the public. From a small beginning in a caboose, the ridership neared 100,000 by the end of the 1960s. Many new slogans now appeared to entice travelers aboard, including the "Matchless Travel Adventure" into "yesteryear." Enthusiastic rail fans spread the word, and the railroad did more promoting despite still claiming that it was not in the tourist business.

Yet problems persisted. Arthur Ballantine, and all Durangoans, were very familiar with the possibility of a flood. They had only recently gone through it. The Animas River flooded in September 1970, bringing back memories, to old-timers, of the 1911 "flood of the century." The railroad stopped running,

and Amos Cordova explained. "Mile-wise there was probably about five or six total miles that were destroyed. But they were destroyed so bad that it washed away the road bed and left the rails and the ties hanging precariously."

Some Durangoans thought that flood might mark the end of the Silverton train. Others speculated that the road bed might make a "spectacular" mountain road. Not so. The railroad promised that, despite the rebuilding needed and the expense involved, the line would return to service "one more time." That last statement, as would be imagined, worried locals, along with the fact that the railroad seriously considered selling, if a buyer could be found.

Despite all these tribulations, when the train reopened after the 1970 flood it proved more popular than ever.

As Colorado neared the state's centennial year, 1976, the potential sale of the railroad, which had now become a major tourist attraction, continued to linger in the background. In an October interview that year, Chamber of Commerce director C.R. Ellsworth raised a concern that persisted on many people's minds: "Well, of course, how many more years can a 100 year old train run?" He went on, "We're real proud of what the Denver & Rio Grande has done and is doing. But again at the same time we know that maybe there is something we should be doing to get ready for anytime that this [abandonment] might happen."

Despite overall progress on several transportation and tourist fronts, the D&RGW wanted to sell its isolated railroad line. The changing world of late twentieth-century railroading was not conducive to an isolated, short narrow gauge line cut off from the railroad's main routes. With increasing numbers of passengers, the line was more attractive to potential buyers than ever before.

Buyers appeared to be interested. Longtime employee Cordova recalled showing some of them around. But the Rio Grande wanted money up front, not a pay as you go plan. Profitability as a traditional rail line was no longer feasible, so they recognized that finding a new owner would entail promoting the heritage of the Durango-to-Silverton train. The line could only make money if the new owner focused on the railroading mystique and legacy of an earlier age.

As Durango celebrated its 100-year birthday and the centennial of the train's arrival, 1980-81, the D&RGW announced the sale of the line. On March 25, 1981, Florida businessman and railroad enthusiast Charles Bradshaw became the new owner. Finally, the Denver & Rio Grande bid adieu to its narrow gauge heritage. Eventually, its tracks all but gone, its name would be all that remained in the annals of American railroading.

Bradshaw quickly brought innovations to the line, including winter trains, heightened promotion, "new" equipment, and an increase in the number of trains during the summer season. On February 10, 1989, he and the train suffered a major setback – the roundhouse burned. Amos Cordova remembered it vividly.

> We had six locomotives in there in different phases of being repaired because that's our down time for repair of our locomotives. The fire department claimed the fire was approximately 2,000 degrees Fahrenheit at the ceiling point. Of course, all the ceiling and roof fell on top of the six locomotives.
>
> We're talking about the most severe damage being caused in the cabs, where you have all the knobs and all the steam gauges, and all the clamping, and so forth. All that was totally destroyed.

It was a setback, certainly, but with determination and drive, the round-house was rebuilt – the first one known to have been built since 1906. The locomotives were repaired by the time of the spring opening in 1990.

The rebuilt roundhouse contained eight storage stalls and offered modern facilities in every way possible, while keeping the nineteenth century look. Here the work would be done – repairs, and year-round maintenance, plus the monthly inspections – that kept these "mature" engines chugging back and forth. The construction and repair shops built and restored cars, and, all told, did the work that allowed the trains to continue running. Amos Cordova described the broadened scope of that work. "We are restoring cars for other people, doing outside work for other companies. We are the biggest one in this particular area that can do that."

In one respect, the fire "actually benefitted the railroad," he said, adding, "Prior to the 1989 fire, we didn't have the facilities that we have now." The public also could tour the facilities and learn about the railroad's history and heritage, adding further to their visit.

What some people consider progress had become a challenge for the railroad as well. Durango had changed over the decades since World War II. Will Rogers observed back in the thirties that "Durango was out of the way and glad of it," but that no longer held true. Now the community worked to lure tourists. The Chamber of Commerce, in 1969, boasted, "We think Durango has great potential [and] is a great place to live with a pleasant environment." As Robert Redford observed at a 1978 symposium at Vail, "it's insane to assume that we can go forward without development. We are a development-oriented society."

And it happened. The town grew to 15,000 residents, and the valley

Amos Cordova

Six locomotives were heavily damaged in the February 1989 roundhouse fire. Despite the damage, the railroad continued operations that summer.

through which the railroad now had run for over 100 years, blossomed into housing developments. Fewer and fewer people remembered the "olden times," when the Denver & Rio Grande had been the community's lifeline. Newcomers grew to greatly outnumber old-timers and with them came new ideas and new expectations.

Now settled in the valley north of town, newcomers raised a chorus of complaint. Their sense of smell appeared acute, while their understanding of local history and its heritage seemed more than a bit deficient. This smoky train, they claimed, was destroying their beautiful valley and their quality of life. All this, despite the fact that the Environmental Protection Agency stated that the train smoke remained within its clean air standards.

The railroad chugged on, a quaint relic of another age that brought tourists in the summer months and sometimes created a bit of inconvenience as it steamed through town. The late 1980s and 1990s, however, proved years of tribulation for the railroad, including issues that were not widely recognized by locals, whether newcomers or old-timers. Tourism, which had boomed, now slowed, and train travel plateaued. Aging equipment required constant maintenance, and new equipment proved too expensive. Other costs increased too.

Durangoans were aware, however, of the railroad's problems with forest and grass fires along the tracks, caused by train engines' hot cinders. Fires had happened ever since the first engine chugged northward, but it came to a head in July 1994, when cinders from the train started the Mitchell Lakes fire. It burned some 270 acres and generated bad publicity for the railroad, which declined to pay the full cost of fighting the fire. The U.S. Forest Service charged the railroad with "negligently causing the fire" and asked the court to order it to pay damages. The railroad denied it was negligent and countered by stating that firefighting costs seemed "unjustifiably high." In the end, Charles Bradshaw reached a negotiated settlement with the Forest Service in federal court in Denver.

Mitchell Lakes was followed by a smaller fire affecting some twenty-five acres in Animas Canyon. Eventually, the railroad started sending "pop" cars after every train, carrying firefighting equipment to put out any grass fires before they could grow larger. Every train also included a baggage car to carry water and firefighting equipment.

Rumors surfaced that the railroad had, again, been placed on the market. They proved true on March 17, 1997. An announcement confirmed that First American Railroad, Inc., an "entertainment-based passenger rail company," had purchased the line. Bradshaw expressed great confidence in the Hollywood, Florida, company which was building a luxury "fun" train to run from Fort Lauderdale to Orlando. However, the company did not get off to a good start when the round-trip fares jumped from $42 to $49, the first increase in three years. The company justified the increase by saying that "traditionally, fare hikes have come about every three years." If nothing else, it proved a bad publicity move locally, because 1996 had been a "down" tourist year. The railroad, one of Durango's tourist pillars, had not helped by raising fares.

From that point, the state of affairs worsened. Matters deteriorated throughout the next year over the possibility of the train not going into downtown Silverton. Rather, it would stop at the depot, where it was rumored a "frontier town" would be built. This was followed by a flap over a comment by the company president that "Silverton can be the Williamsburg, Virginia, of Western mining towns if they put their minds to it." Silvertonians had no intention of putting their minds to it.

Nor were things going well in Florida for the hard-pressed First American Railroad. Another rumor surfaced that the company planned to use funds from its Colorado operations to bolster the finances of its Florida train. It was not something locals wanted to hear. Rumors swirling around the company added up to horrible publicity – not good for the railroad's new owner. Meanwhile, relations between Silverton and Durango and the railroad deteriorated to a twentieth-century low.

After one tumultuous year, Al and Carol Harper became owners in 1998. The former First American chairman and chief executive officer promptly moved to improve public relations at both ends of the line. He succeeded through holding public meetings, showing a willingness to listen, working with the two communities and, most importantly, exhibiting a deep appreciation for the history and heritage of the railroad and its role in southwestern Colorado.

By then, environmentalism and "quality of life" had become catch phrases among Americans and Durangoans, and the railroad received no immunity from such concerns or criticism. For south Durango residents, concerns focused on the coal smoke that settled in the evening over their section of town, as the boilers were kept hot for the next day's trains. For the rest of the century – and into the next – the issue festered. In response to concerns, the railroad held public meetings and tried a variety of approaches to resolve the smoke issue. It was finally decided to use wood pellets rather than coal to keep the boilers hot. A Train Smoke Mitigation Task Force was also organized to discuss ways to cut emissions.

The issue, while quiet, still is a potential flash point for the Durango & Silverton. Recommendations included using diesel instead of coal-fired locomotives for all switching and track maintenance in Durango. Proponents believed these measures would help ameliorate the concerns.

As the century closed and a new millennium opened, Harper stabilized the situation, promoted better community relations, and put the Durango-to-Silverton back on track. He held special events for children, families and groups and opened a museum with exhibits for all ages. New train cars and other innovations appeared and the railroad once more became a positive factor in Silverton and Durango.

Durangoans and Silvertonians breathed a sigh of relief, and the railroad once more assumed the role of a good neighbor to both communities. As one resident of Durango confidently pointed out, "In spite of whatever happens to the ownership . . . I think this railroad will run in spite of itself."

Happily, that bridge has never had to be crossed, and the Durango-to-Silverton is chugging confidently along in the twenty-first century.

Durango & Silverton Narrow Gauge Railroad

Following the 1989 fire, the roundhouse was rebuilt and expanded within a year. The right half of the building now houses a museum with an ever-changing display of cars and locomotives that remain in use.

Summer

Summer in the San Juans is a season of burgeoning possibilties. Waterfalls thunder as snowmelt strains the banks of the Animas River. Leaves burst forth on the trees and colorful wildflowers blanket the mountains. The cold winter months are a distant memory as elk trudge back to the high country and bears emerge from their dens in search of grubs under fallen trees. Skis and snowshoes are replaced with backpacks, hiking poles, and paddles.

The tracks have been cleared of snow, both what fell from the heavens and what roared down the steep mountainsides that tower over them. The cars have been refurbished; the locomotives have started making the 3,000-foot climb to Silverton. A constant jangle of ringing phones pervades the ticket office in the Durango depot, as people from all over the world clamor for the opportunity to ride the historic rails through what many consider the most beautiful mountains anywhere on the planet.

Like the black bears, Silverton has awakened from its winter slumber. Shop owners have washed windows and restocked their shelves. Restaurateurs have menus and meals ready. The sidewalks are filling with throngs of visitors. The train has returned! Just as the arrival of the first Denver & Rio Grande train was celebrated in 1882, the return of the Durango & Silverton is a joyous day in this mountain hamlet.

The season starts with a blessing from the region's early inhabitants, the Southern Utes. In traditional regalia, they dance and bless the train as it departs from Durango, and again when it arrives at Cascade Canyon. Along the way, they talk with passengers about their Shining Mountains and centuries-old Ute culture.

Thomas the Tank Engine™ comes to town soon after, to the delight of throngs of children and their parents. In the coming months, the Lone Ranger and Tonto will save train passengers from would-be "bandits" and celebrants will ride the rails to Silverton to watch Independence Day fireworks ringed by jagged mountain peaks. Outdoor enthusiasts will hitch a ride to the edge of the Weminuche Wilderness, where they'll trek on the Colorado Trail, climb 14,000-foot peaks, and share the terrain with moose, mountain goats, and marmots. Others will raft the Animas River rapids. Adventurers will soar through the trees on a series of steel cables at Tall Timber, each flight more thrilling than the last.

In August, railroad fans will flock to Durango and Silverton for Railfest, riding historic trains and pop cars on the D&SNGRR rails as they immerse themselves in their love of all things train.

Few who board the trains will realize all that is going on behind the scenes to make their adventures possible. Right-of-way maintenance crews constantly survey the tracks, making repairs as necessary and clearing any hazards. Others follow the trains, extinguishing any cinder-caused fires along the route. Roundhouse crews and car men work all night making any needed repairs on the century-old steam-powered locomotives and cars, keeping wood pellet fires burning in them all night so they'll be ready for coal in the morning. Concession car workers, premium car attendants and gift shop clerks make sure they have everything in stock for passengers' comfort and enjoyment. Railroad staff arranges for special trains for everything from weddings to private parties.

Over the boisterous months of summer, thousands will respond to the conductor's call: All Aboard! ➤➤

Yvonne Lashmett

Marc Saphir

Yvonne Lashmett

Marc Saphir

Marc Saphir

Yvonne Lashmett

workin' on the railroad

"What started as a seasonal summer job in 1985 has turned into a passion. Steam railroading really does get in your blood! It has been passed to my grandchildren who now have it in their blood and look forward to every train ride! "

– Yvonne Lashmett
Employee since 1985
marketing specialist

Darel Crawford

Seasons of the Narrow Gauge   **23**

Top right: Gondolas, seen here on the High Bridge, are especially popular during the warm summer months.

Bottom left: Watercolor painter Rusty Steel was a fixture at the Durango depot for many years.

Lower right: Passengers in wheelchairs ride in comfort, thanks to a special lift and floor anchors.

Roy Roberts

Yvonne Lashmett

Yvonne Lashmett

Seasons of the Narrow Gauge   **25**

Dot Bodiroga shows Jacy Jackson the view from the Harper family's private car, the General Palmer. Jacy is the daughter of Jeff Jackson, D&SNGRR senior vice president.

Marc Saphir

Warren Levingston

"If you love your job,
you never have to work a day in your life."

– **Jeff Ellingson**
Employee since 1984
car shop, museum curator

Yvonne Lashmett

Left: Frank Cianci
Center: Jeff Ellingson
Right: Bill Colley

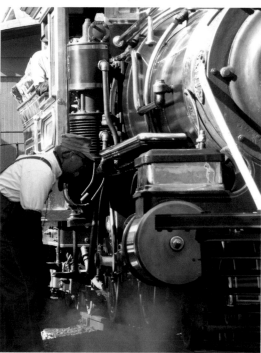

Warren Levingston

A Southern Ute dancer performs the blessing of the D&SNGRR before departing the Durango depot.

Marc Saphir

Far left: Eddie Box Jr. looks out at the Highline.

Above: Southern Utes talk with passengers in the Prospector car about their tribe's long history in the San Juan Mountains.

Left: Children share the special blessing day at Cascade Canyon.

Seasons of the Narrow Gauge   **29**

Yvonne Lashmett

The D&SNGRR fulfilled six-year-old Wyatt Tietz's wish to see the Narrow Gauge. During their visit, the Cedaredge, Colorado, family was able to meet the entire train crew. Wyatt was especially thrilled to tour the locomotive with his father Dan, guided by engineer Bill Colley.

Yvonne Lashmett

Barry J. Durand

Yvonne Lashmett

Day Out with Thomas is a popular
family event each June.

Yvonne Lashmett

Seasons of the Narrow Gauge **31**

Yvonne Lashmett

Yvonne Lashmett

Top left and right: Lone Ranger and
Tonto ride to the rescue, then parade
the desperados by passengers during
a stop in the Animas Valley.

Right: Participants in the Cowboy
Gathering entertain riders on a
special train.

Yvonne Lashmett

Marc Saphir

Seasons of the Narrow Gauge **33**

In addition to moving cars
around in the train yard,
diesels are used to
pull special and
unscheduled trains.

Gerald Baumann

Marc Saphir

Seasons of the Narrow Gauge **35**

Yvonne Lashmett

Yvonne Lashmett

Outdoor enthusiasts, including boaters, hikers, and Tall Timber soarers, use the train to reach remote areas of the San Juan National Forest.

Yvonne Lashmett

Yvonne Lashmett

As waterfalls dwindle from torrents to trickles, the river becomes more hospitable to kayakers and rafters.

Marc Saphir

Marc Saphir

Marc Saphir

Gerald Baumann

Rail Rangers, volunteers for the
U.S. Forest Service and
Bureau of Land Management,
answer passengers' questions about
plants, wildlife, mining, local history,
geology, and more.

Elizabeth A. Green

Passengers on the Independence Express celebrate the 4th of July in Silverton and return to Durango after the fireworks show.

July 26, 2010, two rock slides at Milepost 492.5 (Snowshoe Slide) buried the track and dammed the Animas River, blocking trains from reaching Silverton. Maintenance of Way crews responded immediately and service to Silverton was resumed the next day.

Denny Beggrow

Linda Pampinella

Left: A July 2007 rock slide buried the tracks at Milepost 485.4 (No-Name Slide).

Above: As part of its fire prevention program, every train is followed by a pop car with water and equipment to extinguish any hot spots from cinders.

Bill Ramaly

Marc Saphir

Marc Saphir

Held in mid-August every year, Railfest attracts trains and fans from the U.S. and other countries.

Opposite page: The wood-burning Eureka, comes from Reno, Nevada, for Railfest.

Left: Three trains stop for photographers at the Elk Park wye during Railfest.

Below: Volunteers and passengers help load wood to fuel the Eureka for a trip to Silverton.

John Ninnemann

Gerald Baumann

Linda Pampinella

Yvonne Lashmett

Top left: The Rio Grande Southern Railroad built seven Galloping Goose motor cars in the 1930s to haul passengers and freight.

Bottom left: Galloping Goose crosses the High Bridge

Top right: The Casey Jones rail car is owned by the San Juan County Historical Society.

Opposite page: Railfest provides an opportunity for private pop car owners to travel the route through the San Juan Mountains.

Seasons of the Narrow Gauge   **45**

Darel Crawford

Opposite page: Locomotives pose for photographers in the train yard; the roundtable can be seen at lower right, and the roundhouse left center.

This page: Members of a local Harley owners group pose for a club photo at the Durango depot.

Marc Saphir

In celebration of the railroad's 125th anniversary, descendants of homesteaders who had settled around Durango by 1881 were guests of the railroad on a special trip to Cascade Canyon, where they were served a buffet lunch.

Yvonne Lashmett

Gary Dawson

Seasons of the Narrow Gauge   **49**

"I love being outside.
My office is up in the national forest,
and you can't beat that."

– Robert Manore
Employee since 1992
worked up from laborer to Maintenance of Way foreman

Yvonne Lashmett

Seasons of the Narrow Gauge   **51**

Fall

Labor Day signals a change in the San Juans. Nights turn cold, and passengers arrive at the depot wearing extra layers of clothing. Soon, frost will sparkle in the early morning as trains make their way through the Animas Valley.

The river is tamed, at least in comparison to the rowdy months of spring and summer when rafts and kayaks maneuvered through its non-stop rapids. Now the clear green water invites passengers to try to spot the trout that inhabit its chilly depths.

In this magnificent region, it is difficult to pick a favorite season. But many would assert that nothing beats fall, when the aspens blanket the mountains with a mosaic of greens, golds, pinks, and occasional reds. Add those few days when gambel oaks join the show with their burgundies, oranges, and scarlets, and few would disagree that color season is magnificent.

Photographers welcome the special trains that allow them to get on and off and shoot the train against a colorful backdrop. Days of preparation go into every season's photographers' trains. Locations have to be scouted, not only for their scenic beauty, but also for their safety. Engineers oblige with extra blasts of steam and smoke, backing up the train, then moving forward past the incessantly clicking cameras.

Fall festivals in Durango include special trains. Many of the best cowboy poets in the country gather in late September to share their distinctive and delightful Old West verse. Passengers on trains bound for Cascade Canyon will be treated to live performances, then a barbecue at the Cascade Pavilion, where they'll hear even more of this authentic Western art form.

Then Durango's founding days will come to life with a host of activities featuring people in Victorian and Old West costumes. Living up to those frontier traditions, special heritage trains will feature outlaws along with the respectable ladies and gents of days gone by. Passengers can prepare by buying "gold" and "silver" coins at the depot to appease the desperados – all for a good cause, as proceeds benefit a local non-profit.

As leaves fade and drop and snow graces the mountain peaks, children gather to pick pumpkins, play games, take a hay ride, and cozy up to Charlie Brown, Lucy, and Snoopy. Dressed in colorful costumes, families board the train for their trip to the Peanuts™ Great Pumpkin Patch, where an afternoon of fun is topped off by selecting their very own pumpkins.

Meanwhile, another group of special passengers welcomes the opportunity to ride into the high country. By taking the train, hunters and outfitters spare themselves countless hours of trekking over rough terrain to reach their hunting camps. And those who are successful haul their bounty out in the D&SNGRR baggage car.

As snow falls on the high country, it is time to bid farewell to Silverton for awhile. Not everyone will close for the winter, but many business owners and employees welcome the opportunity to take a break after another successful season.

It is time, too, for the Durango & Silverton to take a break. Locomotives and cars go into the maintenance shop or car barn for some intense TLC. Track crews replace ties and rails where needed. Depot facilities are spruced up.

And very soon, trains will be back on the rails for a magical trip to the North Pole. ➸

Marc Saphir

Roy Roberts

Yvonne Lashmett

Linda Pampinella

Marc Saphir

Darel Crawford

"I love the railroad for what it does for Durango and the community. Think what a different place it would be if the railroad had been abandoned like so many others were. I can't imagine the difference it would make for Silverton. It would barely be on the map. What a loss that would be."

– **Charley Gremmels**

Darel Crawford

The train crosses the Animas River
five times on its journey from
Durango to Silverton.

John Ninnemann

Right: Hunters and outfitters use the train to access remote locations.

Below: The locomotive blows steam as it rolls through Elk Park for a line of photographers.

Linda Pampinella

Yvonne Lashmett

"It gets really busy in the roundhouse when they get back from Silverton. They'll have repairs to do, parts to make, so the trains can go back to Silverton tomorrow."

– Jeff Ellingson

Darel Crawford

Marc Saphir

A slow spin on the turntable changes
direction for locomotives and cars as
they enter and leave the roundhouse.

Marc Saphir

Seasons of the Narrow Gauge   **59**

The dispatcher is key to safe operations, controlling all traffic on the entire route from the Durango depot to downtown Silverton, including passenger and work trains, as well as pop cars.

Marc Saphir

B. Hanes

Left: At the end of another trip, a workman empties firebox contents into the ash pit before the locomotive goes to the roundhouse.

Top right: Spare parts line the edge of the train yard.

Bottom right: Trains move around the yard on a network of interconnected tracks.

Marc Saphir

Marc Saphir

Yvonne Lashmett

Left: A giant jack-o'-lantern at the depot announces the pumpkin patch is open for business.

Below: Costumed children and their families ride a special train to the patch, where they play games and take a hay ride.

Yvonne Lashmett

Yvonne Lashmett

Yvonne Lashmett

Above: Families line up, pumpkins in hand, for the return trip to Durango.

Right: Railroad employees and their families honor our military in the Durango Veterans Day parade.

Yvonne Lashmett

Yvonne Lashmett

Left: Outlaws appear in many costumes on the Heritage Train.

Below: Passengers enjoy music and poetry at the Cascade Canyon Wye, as part of the Cowboy Gathering.

Linda Pampinella

Yvonne Lashmett

Barry J. Durand

Yvonne Lashmett

Weddings on the train are a special occasion, whether they are planned, like the marriage of Amanda Peacock and Gary Tuttle on July 17, 2004, or spontaneous like the one described on the facing page that started at the Needleton Tank.

Yvonne Lashmett

"On October 8, 2009, I was a brakeman on the train, along with Mike Nichols and Bob Kuhn. A gentleman told me he was going to ask his girl-friend to marry him at Needleton tank on the way down to Durango. When we stopped for water, I cleared the Cinco platform for him, and as soon as she said "yes," I ripped open a flare and started flashing it back and forth. At that point, Mike said that as a conductor he was able to marry people on the train. So we quickly went into high gear and put on an amazing wedding on the Cinco at the Highline horseshoe curve. Dot Bodiroga, the Cinco attendant, drew up a beautiful wedding certificate. I made a veil with receipt tape from the concession car. We stopped at Tall Timber and Denny Beggrow helped us pick flowers for a bouquet. The concession car workers, Cathy Haviland and Mary Lynn Hastings, are beautiful singers, so they sang for the bride and groom. I was maid of honor, Bob was best man and Mike married them. A couple on the Cinco gave them their 100-calorie carrot cakes for wedding cake. And the coolest part was when Mike radioed the engineer, Bill Colley, to tell him they were holding a wedding, Bill played the whole wedding march on the train whistle."

– J. Leigh Mestas
Employee since 1994
concessions, private car attendant, brakeman

Roy Roberts

Erik Nelsen

Erik Nelsen

Erik Nelsen

Erik Nelsen

Top left: A speedswing is used to remove a large boulder that had fallen on the tracks.

Top right: A flooding creek threatens to wash out the tracks in October 2006.

Left: The Maintenance of Way crew works through the night to clear a rock slide and repair any damage to the tracks.

Marc Saphir

Steam-powered locomotives are not turned "off" at night. The roundhouse crew works on them all night, not only keeping wood pellet fires going in them (scrubbers capture and clean the smoke), but also taking care of any problems that occurred that day. Early in the morning, long before passengers arrive at the depot, they oil each locomotive, then move it onto the turntable. Once on the track, it is driven forwards and backwards to assure everything is working properly, and only after it has passed all the inspections will it proceed onto the main track ready for another run.

Marc Saphir

Marc Saphir

"Mother Nature always has something
different coming at us.
Not one day is ever the same."

– **Robert Manore**

Darel Crawford

Darel Crawford

Winter

For six weeks each winter, the San Juan Mountains become the backdrop for the North Pole. Children decked out in their pajamas and warm jackets will climb aboard the Durango & Silverton for a magical trip on the Polar Express.

As the train wends its way through town, they'll sip hot cocoa, munch on cookies, sing Christmas carols, and listen to the story of a little boy's encounter with Santa Claus. Elves and St. Nick himself will greet them as they reach their destination, where trees festooned with colorful lights cast brilliant reflections on freshly fallen snow. As they return to the depot, children will clutch precious silver bells and perhaps nod off to sleep, their dreams filled with the joy and wonder of the season.

Black bears will be bedded down for the winter when trains return to the rails for a daily trip to Cascade Canyon, deep in the San Juan National Forest. Passengers may glimpse other high country wildlife along the way, especially elk and bighorn sheep. At Cascade, they'll be welcomed with a roaring fire in the pavilion. The more adventurous folks will follow a trail through the woods to a bridge spanning the Animas River.

Railroad workers clear snow off the tracks after every storm, so that trains can travel to the mythical North Pole, or venture into the mountains. Locomotives are outfitted with plow blades for the small jobs, and heavy-duty equipment is called into action for deep snow. A flanger behind the locomotive widens the path and clears between the rails. A flatbed car hauls a snowblower and bulldozer for heavy-duty work. At the back of the work train is a caboose, where the eight-man crew can prepare their meals, rest, and warm up in front of a coal stove.

Like so many of the working components of the Durango & Silverton, when not in use, the caboose is on display in the roundhouse museum. In late November, the museum takes on a festive air as it fills with decorated trees donated by area businesses. The trees are auctioned off to benefit Community Connections.

This is the season when year-round employees often change hats. Brakemen become mechanics and firemen become track-layers. With only one daily train after December, winter is the time for deep maintenance. Locomotives are opened up and checked, from their tubes and boilers to their wheel sets, bearings, and brakes. New parts are milled in the machine shop, which is capable of making practically any part. After the roundhouse burned in 1989, then-owner Charles Bradshaw scoured the country in search of equipment for rebuilding train components. Thus, the catastrophe became a path to self-sufficiency for the railroad.

Periodically, each locomotive is completely torn down and rebuilt. Where metal has worn thin, it is replaced. New fire bricks are installed.

Cars are refurbished with new paint, wallpaper, and fixtures as needed. New cars are built, like the popular Silver Vista. Others are converted, like the coach that was refitted as the Prospector, complete with an enlarged version of the D&SNGRR route map on its ceiling.

In the depot's upstairs offices, employees are hard at work planning for the coming year. They sort out the schedules, pull together the myriad loose ends, develop new specialty trains and tour packages, and the marketing materials to promote them. And they compile the newest edition of *All Aboard*, the D&SNGRR publication.

Only the bears have been asleep. Come spring, the fruits of everyone's labors will be evident for all. ➤➤

Marc Saphir

Yvonne Lashmett

Yvonne Lashmett

Marc Saphir

Yvonne Lashmett

Roy Roberts

workin' on the railroad

"I like being an engineer. This is where my heart is. I like the machine itself – it's almost like it's human. The steam locomotive is an extension of the engineer's skills. It responds to the individual touch of each engineer."

– Mike Nichols
Employee since 1994
engineer, brakeman, conductor

Maryanne Nelson

Seasons of the Narrow Gauge **77**

Yvonne Lashmett

Yvonne Lashmett

The D&SNGRR brings the beloved story of the Polar Express to life for thousands of children and their families each winter.

Kathy Myrick

Yvonne Lashmett

80 Winter

Yvonne Lashmett

The auction of beautifully decorated trees and wreaths culminates a four-day celebration, which raises more than $30,000 to help people with developmental disabilities.

Yvonne Lashmett

Marc Saphir

The Cascade Canyon train takes passengers into a winter wonderland. School groups travel for a special rate, and participate in learning activities designed by Fort Lewis College.

Marc Saphir

Gerald Baumann

Yvonne Lashmett

Seasons of the Narrow Gauge   **83**

Volunteers help passengers at trackside and assist with special events. In appreciation, they are the guests in premium cars on the Cascade Canyon train.

Marc Saphir

Snowdown, Durango's annual winter festival, includes a light parade and a hot air balloon launch.

Seasons of the Narrow Gauge   **85**

Yvonne Lashmett

Yvonne Lashmett

Yvonne Lashmett

Workers scout locations and tramp down snow, so photographers can get the perfect shot of the Narrow Gauge steaming through the San Juan Mountains.

Seasons of the Narrow Gauge **87**

Marc Saphir

Marc Saphir

Top left: Robert Manore

Bottom left: Steve Waisura

Right: Rich Millard, chief conductor operates the hand brake on a boxcar.

Opposite page: The winter photographer's train crew includes, back, Gary Saltsman; front, from left, Mike Nichols, Dot Bodiroga, Bill Colley, Rich Millard, Bruce Anderson (a volunteer) and Erik Nelsen.

Gerald Baumann

Gerald Baumann

A work train steams into the mountains to move snow, complete with plow blade on the locomotive, flanger, bulldozer on the flatbed, and two cabooses for the crew. Crews generally return to Durango at the end of each day, rather than risk being caught in an avalanche overnight.

Darel Crawford

Darel Crawford

Marc Saphir

Marc Saphir

Marc Saphir

Oppostie page, top left: Flanger

Bottom left: The crew moves the tank car from the siding where it is stored at Rockwood.

Top right: A cart has to be moved so that snow can be cleared from the siding as well as the main tracks.

Bottom right: The locomotive and flanger clear snow off the tracks.

This page, bottom: The snowblower follows the train, moving remaining snow off the High Bridge.

Right:The excavator clears the Highline.

Marc Saphir

Marc Saphir

workin' on the railroad

"I love clearing avalanches in the winter. I fly in the helicopter and show the pilots all the chutes that run over the tracks. We go to the top of the mountains, then drop 50-pound bombs into the slides and get them to run."

–**Robert Manore**

Right: After big storms, a work train must clear the way before the Cascade Canyon train goes out. The work crew pictured here includes, left to right, front, Josh Levine, Dan Stine, Leon Montoya, Mike May, Gary Saltsman; rear, Bill Colley, Steve Waisura (back), Moe Rael

Below: Blowing snow can obscure the engineer's view.

Marc Saphir

Marc Saphir

Marc Saphir

Workers take a welcome break in
the caboose after long hours of
pushing snow.

Marc Saphir

Marc Saphir

Seasons of the Narrow Gauge   **97**

Marc Saphir

Top left: Beginning in late fall, locomotives go into the shop for deep maintenance. After 1,472 days of service, a locomotive must be thoroughly inspected. The "skin" is removed so all components and fittings can be examined for signs of wear or weakness, a process that takes 2,000 to 4,000 man-hours.

Bottom left: Wheel trucks are removed and repaired or replaced, along with all other working parts.

Bottom right: New tubes are installed in the boiler as needed.

Marc Saphir

Marc Saphir

Marc Saphir

When locomotives undergo deep maintenance in the roundhouse, the fronts are opened so mechanics can inspect and clean the boiler tubes. Wheel sets are pulled and re-trued. Parts are inspected for signs of wear. Mechanics even crawl into the firebox to examine the bricks and metal. If new parts are needed, the machine shop manufactures them.

Marc Saphir

Marc Saphir

Yvonne Lashmett

Like the locomotives and cars, the historic D&SNGRR depot is refurbished during the winter.

"I'm the painter. If it looks good, it's my fault and if it looks bad, it's my fault."

– Greg Simpson
Employee since 2002
paint shop, construction, museum

631

Marc Saphir

John Ninnemann

The car barn crew is able to make any wooden parts, rebuild wheel sets, refurbish car interiors, hang wallpaper, and paint all train components.

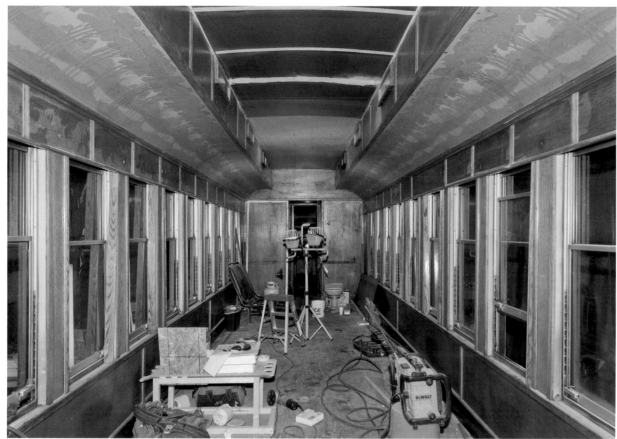

Marc Saphir

Left: A standard coach is being modified to serve as the Prospector deluxe class car. It can accommodate tables and chairs, or be reconfigured for serving buffet meals.

Below: Passengers on a special train enjoy a buffet meal in the Prospector car.

Marc Saphir

Marc Saphir

A crew is building track sections for the events park that will be located in the Animas Valley. The sections will be transported to the site on a flatbed car and assembled there. Once completed, the new park will be used for many of the special event trains.

Opposite page: A work train hauls materials and equipment for repairing the track.

Marc Saphir

Seasons of the Narrow Gauge

Spring

Springtime in the San Juans is a season of anticipation. After months of snow and cold, people and animals alike are hoping for warm sun, green grass, and flowers. Rock peeks through the deep layers of snow that have covered it all winter. Fresh shoots appear on the trees and shrubs. Having depleted their winter larders, squirrels and chipmunks scurry about in search of food.

The spring break crowds come to slide down slopes of corn snow and revel in the cobalt blue skies overhead. Passengers on the Cascade Canyon train become witnesses to the transformation as the river turns from clear green to café au lait brown, swelling with early snowmelt.

Across the country and abroad, people are planning their summer vacations. What visit to Southwest Colorado would be complete without riding the train and touring Mesa Verde National Park? Reservations start pouring in for families, individuals, and tour groups. History comes alive on the Durango & Silverton, and they want to experience it.

Preparation is the partner of anticipation on the Narrow Gauge. Bulldozers begin clearing debris-filled snowslides that have buried the tracks between Cascade and Silverton. Helicopters and dynamite may be deployed if the snow is unusually deep, or still clings to the mountainsides waiting for a few more sunny days before it runs to the valley floor. Winter damage to the tracks is repaired. Seasonal employees begin their training, as the ranks nearly double from the less than 100-strong winter work force.

Before their work is finished, a Blues Train will carry fans and performers to Cascade Canyon, where they will fill the crisp mountain air with music and enthusiastic applause. Charlie Brown and his Peanuts™ friends will return with delightful Easter Beagle baskets and fun on the train.

Up in the mountains, hardy Silvertonians welcome their friends and neighbors who traveled south for the winter and begin preparations for another tourist season. And in Durango, Narrow Gauge Day – or Hot Dog Day, as it's fondly known – dawns at the depot. It is a welcome celebration of springtime, with free hot dogs for all, entertainment by the beloved Bar D Wranglers, and special visits by Snoopy, Charlie Brown, and Lucy.

The locomotives chuff out of the roundhouse, go through their morning safety check, and pull out onto the main tracks. Decked out with American flags, they back up to be coupled with the cars they will pull to Silverton. Gondolas and coaches are followed by premium cars, their attendants in bright red or gray vests.

The dispatcher gives the go-ahead, and service to Silverton resumes. There may be snow bridges still spanning the river in places, and flurries may fill the air in Silverton, but spring has definitely arrived.

Forty years ago, two brothers – one a cyclist and the other a D&SNGRR engineer – made a bet on who could reach Silverton first. The cyclist won, as have thousands since that first year. Reaching Silverton in a little over two hours, the pros beat the train handily. Yet even those who arrive long after the train take justifiable pride in having climbed and descended two mountain passes to reach Silverton, nearly 3,000 feet higher than their starting point.

The cyclists' arrival in Silverton is a signal, as clear as the conductor's "All Aboard." Summer has arrived, and another year in the seasons of the Narrow Gauge is about to begin. ➤➤

Yvonne Lashmett

Marc Saphir

Marc Saphir

Al Olson

Yvonne Lashmett

Darel Crawford

workin' on the railroad

"My favorite job is shoveling coal as a fireman. I really enjoy the challenge and the forced workout it gives you, and knowing your back's carrying this train to Silverton."

– Jarrette Ireland
Employee since 2003
fireman, brakeman

Barry J. Durand

Seasons of the Narrow Gauge   **111**

Snowstorms are common in the San Juans throughout the spring months.

Yvonne Lashmett

Marc Saphir

Marc Saphir

In preparation for resuming service to Silverton, crews must clear deep accumulations of snow and debris from slide areas. The work can be treacherous, as equipment climbs steep snowbanks on the edge of the Animas River. All workers wear avalanche beacons so they could be located if caught in a snowslide.

"We go back to avalanche school every year for a refresher class. That's what keeps me going home to my family. It's probably one of the most dangerous jobs out there. Every day we have to be aware of that, be ready for whatever is coming at us."

— **Robert Manore**

Marc Saphir

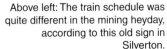
Kathy Myrick

Marc Saphir

Above left: The train schedule was quite different in the mining heyday, according to this old sign in Silverton.

Top right: Passengers book trips and pick up tickets at the ticket window in the Durango depot.

Bottom right: The depot gift shop is stocked and ready for the onslaught of summer visitors.

Marc Saphir

Yvonne Lashmett

John Ninnemann

This page: Narrow Gauge Day. The day before service to Silverton resumes, the whole town is invited to the depot for free hot dogs and entertainment by the Bar D Wranglers.

Facing page: The first train steams through Rockwood on its way to Silverton.

John Ninnemann

Yvonne Lashr

John Ninnemann

Philip Walters

John Ninnemann

Linda Pampinella

Yvonne Lashmett

Jerry Baumann

The Silverton Brass Band welcomes
the first trains of the new season in
early May. Some area residents
celebrate the occasion by dressing in
Victorian attire.

Yvonne Lashmett

Marc Saphir

Seasons of the Narrow Gauge **121**

Waterfalls and creeks fill the Animas River as snow begins to melt in the high country. Track maintenance can be especially challenging this time of year, and freezing temperatures require close monitoring of pipes supplying the water tanks.

Marc Saphir

Yvonne Lashmett

Marc Saphir

Marc Saphir

Top left: Workers lay track for the new events park.

Bottom left: A worker checks a bridge for damage.

Top right: A worker throws the switch so he can move his pop car to a siding before the next train comes through.

Bottom right: Maintenance of Way workers enjoy beautiful scenery in their mountain "office."

Marc Saphir

Seasons of the Narrow Gauge **123**

Top: Train employees join the Iron Horse race to Silverton. Left to right, Ben Barker, Jeff Jackson, Steve Carr, Travis Wheeler, Scott Shewmake. In 40 years of the race, the train has won twice, when cyclists were turned back by blizzards on the passes.

Yvonne Lashmett

Yvonne Lashmett

Yvonne Lashmett

Darel Crawford

Seasons of the Narrow Gauge

Carol Lewin

Yvonne Lashmett

Yvonne Lashmett

Above: The Memorial Day train
honors all branches of the
Armed Forces.

Left: The restored Engine 315 takes
an occasional turn on the tracks.

Members of the North American Rail Car Operators Association ride the Narrow Gauge rails. They must secure permission from the D&SNGRR to run on the tracks and coordinate their trip with the dispatcher in Durango so that they don't interfere with any of the trains.

Barry J. Durand

Seasons of the Narrow Gauge   **127**

Darel Crawford

OUR FIRST 125 YEARS
DEDICATED TO THE EMPLOYEES OF THE D&SNG RAILROAD
THEY MAKE HISTORY COME ALIVE EVERY DAY
MAY THEY BE REMEMBERED FOREVER!!

| EVAN BUCHANAN | PAUL SCHRANCK | | STEVE JACKSON |
| SUPERINTENDENT OF OPERATIONS | VP AND GENERAL MANAGER | VP AND CHIEF MECHANICAL OFFICER | |

BRIAN DAVIES	JAMES MILTON	SCOTTY WEITS	BRANDY WRIGHT	RYAN PRESZLER
JON (ERIK) NELSEN	RANDY BABCOCK	TAMMIE CARTWRIGHT	GARY KEIL	ANDREW ROLLSTIN
ERICK NELSON	LARRY BEAM	RICK PETERSEN	JAMES CARITHERS	KEITH ROSTEN
LEON MONTOYA	STEVEN BELL	KAREN KELLEY	MONTY CAUDLE	DAN STANGBY
BRETT WELLS	STEPHEN CARR	J. LEIGH MESTAS	WILLIAM COLLEY	WAYNE PRATT
MICHAEL RAEL	MARSHALL CHAVEZ	MYRA REJHOLEC	RICHARD MILLARD	KIM JONES
ROBERT MANORE	PHILIP CHEASEBRO	DOT BODIROGA	MICHAEL NICHOLS	DONNA KENNER
ROBERT McCOY	GARY CLARK	TAMMIE HOVET	JEFFREY NORTON	SHARON LOOSE
COLIN BERGQUIST	MIKE CYPHERS	MARY STOFFEL	STEPHEN OTTEN	PAM RAMSEY
TOM VIGIL	BEN FERRN	JOSH MARTIN	DAVID SCHRANCK	JUNE CIANCI
RAY LUDWIG	TONY GARCIA	TARA SHEEHAN	DANIEL SHEWMAKE	SHARON CRAWFORD
JIM MARTINEZ	LEONARD HOFMANN	IRENE BARRY	BEN BARKER	NANCY HOLLAND
SEAN JACKSON	WAYNE KADEMAN	THERESA CASHIO	FRANK CIANCI	LYNN HUTSON
JOHN BERTON	MICHAEL MAHAFFEY	BARBARA HALL	GENE CORRIGAN	SAMANTHA KENNER
JEFF WILBANKS	JOEL MASON	JAMIE PRATT	DUSK EDWARDS	THOMAS BREWER
WESLEY AKERS	CHARLIE MOORE III	JEFF ELLINGSON	JOHN HILLIER	JIM HOLLAND
DAVID ZOOK	ERIC PAUL	JERRY JONES	JARRETTE IRELAND	LESLIE TORBETT
LAWRENCE MUELLER	MARC PERINO	CHARLES JOHNSON	RON KEISER	RICK TURPIN
DAMEN McCADDON	KEVIN SIMMONS	GREG PICARD	PAT KRAMER	CHARLEY GREMMELS
GREG SIMPSON	GARY TOWNE	BOB MORRIS	BOB KUHN	YVONNE LASHMETT
DEREK LaCROIX	DANIEL WEBB	ANDREA SEID	JOSH LEVINE	TILLY MARLMAN
PATRICK LUNA	WILLIAM WHITE	LENDA HINE	RAY LOOSE	MAC PATTERSON
CHRIS MESTAS	TRAVIS WHEELER	CAROL PEACOCK	MIKE MAY	ROBERT MAPLE
ROY McLAUGHLIN	ANN GAIOVNIK	SARAH JAKSHA		

AMERICAN HERITAGE RAILWAYS
LORETTA MURPHY
SR. VICE-PRESIDENT CHIEF FINANCIAL OFFICER
JEFF JACKSON
SR VICE PRESIDENT CHIEF OPERATING OFFICER

ALLEN AND CAROL HARPER
OWNERS
AUGUST 5, 2006

Marc Saphir

D&SNGRR owner Al Harper erected this marker at the Durango depot to honor all who worked for the railroad on its 125th anniversary.

Right: Chief Engineer Steve Otten changes hats for a day to serve as conductor.

Barry J. Durand

"I have been fortunate to meet so many beautiful people – that's what keeps me coming back."

– J. Leigh Mestas

Seasons of the Narrow Gauge   **131**

Marc Saphir

Epilogue

The Future is History

History is a confusing concept. When does history stop and the present begin? Is yesterday's present today's history? And is the future really just historic foresight?

The Durango and Silverton Narrow Gauge Railroad is truly a great American historic treasure. However, unlike historical objects, it is a living, evolving entity. It is not locked into any one historic era, but is ever changing and adapting for a future that ultimately becomes a part of its everlasting heritage.

Confused yet? Well, you can still ride the D&SNGRR just exactly as the miners, settlers, and vagabonds did in 1882. It is historically perfect! But, you can also see small children enjoy "Thomas the Tank," or whole families in pajamas ride "The Polar Express," or have a photo with "Snoopy," or be "held up" by crooks only to be saved by the "Lone Ranger and Tonto." To understand all this, and see the vision for the future for the D&SNGRR, the following topics must be examined:

- ➔ History First and Foremost
- ➔ The Demographics for Success
- ➔ Today is Tomorrow's History
- ➔ Listen to the Market
- ➔ Make History New, Creative and Maybe Even Fanciful
- ➔ The Ultimate Goals

The Philosophy of Ownership

In a sense, the D&SNGRR is not so much owned by individuals, as it is under guardianship by those people who hold the title. As current titleholders, Carol and I strive to be the best stewards of the railroad in its entire 129- year history. We truly understand that the D&SNGRR is a great American treasure and work to ensure that its operation remains true to the way it was run in 1882. You still can ride the train and have the exact experience as those passengers did over a century ago.

We believe in the importance of us all knowing our past. If you want to make sure the American character that made our country the greatest in the world today prospers and continues to grow, we must understand both the

Yvonne Lashmett

Al and Carol Harper

good and the bad that made up our country's heritage. History is the road map to our future. We can only take the right path as a nation in the future if we know from where we came.

In addition to loving history, we strongly believe the best way to preserve history is to make its preservation so interesting and exciting that people will pay a fair price for the experience. That does not mean a historic venue must make a lot of money, but it must be profitable. If you want historic assets to be here for generations to come, it cannot depend on charity or on tax dollars from politicians. It is this philosophy of ownership that guides the D&SNGRR into the future.

History First and Foremost

In operating the Durango and Silverton Narrow Gauge Railroad as a profitable business it would be easy to cheapen the experience and to dilute the historical purity. We could convert the fuel for the steam engines from coal to diesel oil or some other alternative. We could run diesel locomotives on regularly scheduled trips. We could even stop going to Silverton and always turn around at Cascade. That will never happen on our watch.

We cannot tell the "truth" of our history by "faking" how it operates. What makes the D&SNGRR the most significant historic railroad is that its equipment, operation, and route are exactly the same as they have been for 129 years. Anything less is unacceptable. Anything different lacks historical integrity. History must come first and foremost.

The Demographics for Success

The Durango and Silverton Narrow Gauge Railroad is a living entity. The riders of today are not the passengers of yesteryear. There are few miners, prospectors, freight men, sheep herders, or frontier ladies on our current passenger list. As the demographics of ridership change, the railroad must develop markets for new riders.

When we bought the D&SNGRR in 1998, it was easy to see that most passengers on the train were older and that unless something was done, the customer base would die away and the railroad would financially fail. The railroad had to adapt in order to attract young families and children without interrupting its historic scheduled service to Silverton. Thus, the era of special events was born.

The purpose of special events is to introduce new people to the railroad and its history, and to form a wide and long-term customer base. Unless their family is from the "big city," children would normally know little about trains;

much less have ridden one.

"Thomas the Tank" was the D&SNGRR's first family and children's special event. It now draws nearly 5,000 young people annually to the railroad. The next family event added was "The Polar Express." This draws over 17,000 family members each holiday season. We brought in Charlie Brown, Lucy, and Snoopy to draw families for "The Peanuts™ Great Pumpkin Patch Express" and "Peanuts™ Easter Beagle Express" which attract over 7,000 people annually. Soon, the "Lone Ranger" showed up and there are more new family events in the planning stage. All these special events collectively introduce 30,000 people annually to the railroad for short trips and lots of fun activities. And, these special events are profitable. Most important, people learn to love the railroad and then become the future riders to Silverton. The special events will grow in size and variety to ensure a long-term customer interest base and a long-term life for this rail treasure.

Today is Tomorrow's History

Since the Durango and Silverton is not a static display, things are constantly changing. Therefore, what we do today and what happens today, creates tomorrow's history. Some change is beyond the control of ownership and other change is purposeful by ownership.

Nature and government both create change that ownership has nothing to do with. For example, in 2002 a fire destroyed 70,000 acres of forest north of Durango. The railroad was forced to close for 40 days and lost $4,500,000 in that short period of time. As a result, the railroad became expert in fire prevention and suppression. For the first time, diesel locomotives came into service on scheduled runs and maintenance-of-way trips to reduce the chance of sparks emitted from the coal-fired boilers of the steam engines. Tank cars holding 7,000 gallons of water came into use to wet down the right-of-ways on steep grades where steam engines worked hardest, and a box car was added to each passenger consist, carrying 1,000 gallons of water and a water cannon. All onboard crews and MOW workers were trained as efficient firefighters. Nature and government forced this change.

Ownership will make changes as well. New ideas for safety, improvements, and innovations that don't impact historical preservation are always sought. This may become a normal part of the future and it will represent tomorrow's history. Additional changes in gift shop inventory and snack shop menus will reflect the changing wishes of ridership in the future. This change in the future is inevitable, but historically invisible.

Listen to the Market

For the Durango and Silverton Railroad to be successful in the future it must listen to the market. We must make our preservation of history adapt to the demands of the market today. Here are some of those demands:

- Make the experience shorter
- Make the experience fun
- Ensure a sense of value for the money spent
- Provide an optional first-class upgrade
- Demonstrate social consciousness
- Make reservations easy
- Connect to other venues

Some of these demands are tougher than others. All must be addressed one way or another and you must recognize that the future will bring new demands. Here are some of the efforts to meet market demands:

We now have a fleet of seven motor coaches, which means we can reduce a round trip to Silverton by two hours by using a train and motor coach combination. This also increases rail ridership capacity.

Beyond our totally entertaining special events, the D&SNGRR has added on-board Forest Service volunteers who meet and greet riders, telling them of the flora and fauna on the way to Silverton. The railroad has a coloring book as well as a storybook I co-authored entitled *Me and the Bears of Bitter Root*. The story is of a bear encounter that takes place all along the tracks. Further, the D&SNGRR milepost guide is the best in the industry.

The ticket on the train is a true value not only for the ride, but for free entry into a spectacular 18,000-square-foot museum complete with steam engines you can climb on, a model railroad, historic rail cars to tour through, a movie car, and loads of memorabilia to look at. The first firetruck on the Western Slope of the Rockies arrived by rail and is now located in the D&S Museum.

Since we bought the railroad, eight new first-class cars have been added to the rolling stock inventory. This includes a glass-topped gondola car, a family first-class car capable of buffet meals, and two luxury cars serving the Tall Timber Resort. These first-class cars run at an 87 percent load factor, which is generally unheard of in the business.

Yvonne Lashmett

With open sides and glass roof, the Silver Vista provides a panoramic view of the San Juan Mountains.

The D&SNGRR is often questioned about the social and environmental consequences of using coal-fired steam-powered engines. The good news is that a $1,000,000 commitment has erased the carbon footprint of the railroad. We are the only entirely "green" railroad in the world. Here is how it was done:

- Working with Rotary, Kiwanis, and the Lions Clubs, 170 households and businesses in Durango pay a premium on their electric bill to erase the carbon footprint of the entire steam engine fleet.

- Over 3,000 trees have been planted in Durango and the surrounding area to absorb the railroad's CO_2 output.

- A $500,000 scrubber system removes the particulates from the smoke of the engine in the roundhouse.

➤ At night the engines burn reprocessed pelletized sawdust in lieu of coal.

➤ Another $1,000,000 is planned for further smoke reduction. All this means the D&SNGRR is one of the most socially conscious railroads in the world and the future means even greater efforts.

Technology meets history at the D&SNGRR. In 2009 the entire reservation system went online with real-time reservations. Now a customer can go online, select a seat, pay for his ticket, and print his ticket. It is so easy that in the first year nearly 30 percent of riders used the online ticketing system and the percentage grows each year.

Connecting with other venues has grown from only a Mesa Verde National Park tour package to packaging the train with river rafting, four wheeling, snowmobiling, jeep tours, horseback rides and, soon, hotels.

Make History New, Creative and Maybe Even Fanciful

All the previous discourse has been necessary to explain where the D&SNGRR has been in history and how it's changed, in order to explain where will it go in the future. First, there is this guarantee: all regularly scheduled service to Silverton and Cascade Canyon will be powered by coal-fired steam-powered engines. The depot, the equipment, and the operations, will all be historically correct. From there on out, things will change.

The D&SNGRR will be historic, yet every year new and fresh things will happen. There will be new special events, a new car or two added to the fleet annually, new additions to the museum, and new ways to dramatically present history to our customers. Here are some of the fanciful and creative ideas on the drawing board:

❶ Railroad Square will consist of a 220-room hotel, a 22,000-square-foot convention center, and 30,000 square feet of office and retail space devoted to railroad history and culture.

❷ Railroad Park will be a 12.5-acre facility that will serve as a "pumpkin patch" in the fall, the "North Pole" at Christmas, and a close encounter with Colorado wildlife and Smoky Bear in the summer.

❸ A second Silver Vista glass dome car will be built.

❹ There will be an annual Harley-Davidson train to Silverton.

❺ We will have a "Blue Goose" transit trolley on the D&SNGRR tracks in Durango.

❻ Educational and entertaining joint ventures will be established with Fort Lewis College and the Southern Ute Tribe.

❼ A green "super-powered" steam engine will be designed and built to augment the steam engine fleet.

❽ Solar, wind, and other alternative power sources will be developed for all railroad facilities.

❾ New railcamp cars will be developed for overnight wilderness camping on rail sidings.

The future of the D&SNGRR will be one of creativity and excitement.

The Ultimate Goals

So what are the ultimate goals of the Durango and Silverton Narrow Gauge Railroad? It is that this railroad will be preserved and operated for generations to come in its most pure historical fashion. It will appeal to the broadest range of people. It will prosper without charity and without tax dollars. It will educate and entertain. It will be the ultimate historic railroad in the world.

Index

Photographers Index